Parenting with
MERCY

Michelle Brock, M.Ed.

"Bigwig realized that he had stumbled, quite unexpectedly, upon what he needed most of all: a strong, sensible friend who would think on her own account and help to bear his burden."
(from Watership Down)

To my friends who are strong and sensible, share my burdens and tell me when I've got a screw loose, but especially to Deborah, who pestered me when I gave up writing the mercy project until I picked it up again. Then you walked with me until it was finished. Thank you.

Copyright © 2018 by Michelle Elaine Brock

Cover © 2018 by Bretta Watterson

All rights reserved. This book or any portion thereof may not be reproduced without the express written permission of the author except for the use of brief quotations in a book review.

Printed in the United States of America

First Printing, 2018

ISBN 978-0996947732

Scripture taken from the New King James Version®. Copyright © 1982 by Thomas Nelson. Used by permission. All rights reserved.

www.as4me.net

Table of Contents

5   *A Father's Mercy*

13   *Mercy and Repentance*

27   *Mercy and Patience*

41   *Mercy When I Am Offended*

55   *Mercy and Meeting Needs*

73   *Discerning Barriers to Mercy*

87   *Afterword*

1

A Father's Mercy

*Therefore be merciful,
just as your Father also
is merciful. Luke 6:36*

Wʜᴇɴ my firstborn was just a baby, Luke 6:36 caught my attention: "Be merciful, just as your Father also is merciful." I could see it was a direct command, and I wanted to obey it, but I hadn't the foggiest idea how to put it into practice.

Showing mercy is not how we think of Christian parenting. We do not use the word *mercy* often, and when we do, we define it narrowly: "not punishing my children when they deserve it."

Every time I tried showing mercy, I felt guilty. I wanted my children to understand the love and mercy of our great God, but I also knew they needed to learn about the seriousness of sin and God's justice. I was afraid of being inconsistent in my discipline, and showing mercy felt inconsistent. Sometimes, my fear of showing too much mercy caused me to be too harsh!

I tried changing consequences when my instruction had been less than clear or when it seemed my expectations were unrealistic. I wanted to comfort my children after they had been corrected, but I did not want to undermine my correction. Was comforting merciful even though I still corrected my child? Through all my insecurity, Luke 6:36 stuck in my mind and gave me hope that God wanted me to learn how to show mercy to my children, and that doing so would show his character that I longed for them to know.

1. Read Luke 6:27-36. How are God's actions described in verses 35-36?

2. What are the two behaviors in verse 35 that God responds to in mercy?

3. Does the context of Luke 6:36 suggest any more ways we can imitate his mercy?

God's Mercy Is a Father's Mercy

What I really wanted was a verse telling me how and when to show mercy in every situation I encountered. I wanted a verse to tell me when I should show mercy, and when I shouldn't. I did not yet realize that learning to show mercy is like learning wisdom. We first learn principles of mercy; then we must put them into practice.

When Jesus tells us be merciful, like God our Father is merciful, he is identifying a family trait and a practical example of mercy to follow. Just as human families develop a shared culture that can be passed on to others, God's family shares a culture that reflects his nature. How is God merciful? How can I imitate that mercy with others? In Luke 6:36, Jesus could have used the word *King* or *Master* instead of *Father*. Although God is certainly our King and Master, perhaps the best metaphor to showcase mercy is the parenting relationship.

I was intrigued to think about Jesus using the parent and child relationship to highlight God's mercy. This idea was like a seed germinating for the next several years. As I understood more about how he is a merciful Father to me, I became convinced that I should learn how to show mercy to my own children. I decided to start looking to see if the Bible gave reasons for mercy, or if I could find a pattern that I could imitate.

That decision started a search for mercy in my Bible reading that continues to this day. I have learned that, far from subverting our discipline, mercy is a part of Christian discipline itself, not distinct from it. Mercy is integral to what it means to be a Christian parent. My study has changed how I parent my children, and is flowing out in how I love others as well.

4. *What do you know about God's mercy? How have you experienced God's mercy?*
5. *Is the word "mercy" used in our vocabulary when talking about God's daily work in our lives? Why or Why not?*

The Breadth of Biblical Mercy

For awhile, I did not understand much about God's mercy, and I wasn't even sure where to look in the Bible to learn how to be merciful. Every once in awhile, I would read something that challenged me or caused me to think about mercy again, and over time, I started noticing God's mercy in my own life more frequently. I started to gain a better understanding of the many ways I could show mercy to others.

Part of the problem was that I had never thought about God's justice and mercy outside of salvation by grace. When I saw mercy, I put it in the salvation category, something I definitely needed, but a thing so closely related to grace that I might as well just call it grace. What I did not know back then was that the words for *mercy* are distinct from words translated as *grace*.

Our understanding of mercy actually comes from several words translated in English as *pity, compassion, steadfast love, loyal love,* as well as *mercy*. Mercy is a subset of God's love, and often assumes an inequality of some kind. For example, God is infinitely greater than I am; thus, his steadfast love is always merciful. While we love God, our love for God is not considered merciful because he is greater than we are in every way.

The social inequality between a parent and a dependent child is obvious, but sometimes the moral inequality is reversed and I am in need of mercy from them. When I sin against them, they are in the right, and I am wrong. I need their mercy as I recognize my sin and ask forgiveness.

How do we show mercy to peers, whom we normally think of as equals? If a peer has wronged me, showing mercy does not mean I am personally better than she is, but simply that, in this offence, our behavior is unequal. I can show mercy in how I respond. Next week, I may be in the wrong and need her mercy. Furthermore, because we are sinners living among sinners, we will find ourselves giving mercy and in need of mercy regularly!

6. *Matthew 5:7 says, "Blessed are the merciful, for they shall obtain mercy." What comes first in this blessing, giving or receiving mercy?*

7. *Is the mercy we obtain referring to our salvation? Explain your answer.*

Learning Mercy Takes Practice

As I looked for mercy in the Bible, my list of questions grew. Is mercy an emotion or an action? Is it just forgiving others? Why do different translations use such different words to describe this thing that is an attribute of God and something I am supposed to imitate? I started to notice that the Bible used the language of mercy more broadly than I had assumed.

As we look in God's word together, we will see examples of mercy in response to repentance; mercy before repentance, and sometimes mercy responding to a need, and not to sin at all. When we consider all of these examples, we will understand why some consider mercy in the Bible to be part of God's goodness and kindness. God has given us what we need in his word to follow him. When we feel overwhelmed at what we do not know about mercy, we can be confident that guidance exists for us, both in God's word and in the work of the Holy Spirit in our lives.

I often feel awkward trying to show mercy. I have a lot to learn about God's mercy, and I often fall short when I try it out on others. Sometimes I show mercy when I shouldn't, and sometimes I am too harsh when I should be merciful. Thankfully, I have a Heavenly Father who showers me with daily mercy. He reminds me that the practice and struggle to learn is good for me, and I will be better able to show mercy to my children as I learn first hand about his mercy to me.

When God gives us the command to show mercy as our Father is merciful, we do not have the option to ignore it. We might disagree on how and when to apply principles of mercy, but all children of God must consider how to imitate their Father's mercy.

8. *Are you more likely to show too much mercy or too little mercy?*

9. *Have you ever shown mercy when you shouldn't have?*

10. *Have you ever NOT shown mercy when you should have shown it?*

11. *In your action plan at the back of the book, list 2 specific prayer requests about showing mercy. Use the Scripture passages from this chapter for ideas.*

12. *Then list several ways that you may have opportunity in the next week to show mercy.*

2

MERCY AND REPENTANCE

*Now no chastening seems to be joyful for
the present, but painful; nevertheless,
afterward it yields the peaceable fruit
of righteousness to those who have been
trained by it. Hebrews 12:11*

As I TRIED to understand exactly what mercy was, I asked my mentors whether they knew of any verses that could help me to determine when to show mercy. The first Scripture I found came from my mom.

*He who covers his sins will not prosper,
But whoever confesses and forsakes them will
have mercy. Proverbs 28:13*

God shows mercy when we demonstrate a measure of repentance. I love this verse because it connects my actions and God's mercy. I could not apply it to my six-month-old baby, but I saw hope for the future as he grew older. When he became able to own up to his sin, I wanted to imitate God, who responds favorably to humility and confession. Before I was ever able to apply this principle to my children, I spent a great deal of time thinking about this passage and God's mercy to me.

Human nature tends to hide sin and conclude that our problems are caused by confession, not by the sin itself. We think if nobody knows about our sin, we might avoid the consequences; however, God teaches us that doing right by confessing my sin leads to mercy. By faith we understand that hiding sin leads to more problems, not fewer.

Telling the truth about what I have done wrong is particularly difficult. I want to encourage it in my children as much as possible, and I can accomplish this by quickly rewarding truth, instead of reacting harshly to confession.

When my son was still quite young, I noticed him eating in bed and asked him, "What are you eating?" After

Mercy and Repentance

a long pause, he said, "M&Ms...." Sometimes when my children answer truthfully, I'm shocked or horrified, and my emotional response discourages further communication. I could have calmly given consequences, but on this occasion, I reminded him he's not allowed to do that, sent him to put away what he had not eaten, and then considered the matter closed. He was young, and I considered his telling the truth about what he had done wrong to be foundational as I encouraged his repentance. I wanted him to learn that I will respond to an offence differently if he tells the truth about it, just as our God does.

As he matured, I would begin helping him understand more about repentance. Our own understanding of repentance makes a difference in our expectations for our children, and showing mercy is far more manageable when I remember that growth is a long-term process of discipleship. I am looking for direction, not perfection.

James 4:8 says, "Draw near to God and He will draw near to you. Cleanse your hands, you sinners; and purify your hearts, you double-minded." In this passage, James uses the language of motion to discuss our relationship with God. We sometimes rush past without considering what drawing near to God actually looks like. I did, until I had a child ask me what this verse meant. My fumbling attempts to answer her made me realize I knew less than I thought I did.

Drawing near to God seems to be a broad idea that may include many steps in the path of repentance. I am thankful God does not wait to show mercy until I have finally mastered the entire process of repentance. I love knowing God responds to me even when I take small steps toward obedience. One step comes after another. If my criteria for genuine repentance is never repeating another sin, then I am actually putting a burden on my children that God does not place on me.

When my children draw near to God in repentance, they often express a desire to do right. They may ask for prayer or help doing right, but more often are simply responsive when I ask if they are willing to pray together or want help doing right. Repentance sometimes simply means they will notice more quickly when they are in the wrong, and turn around more quickly when they are corrected.

The consequences we give are determined by wisdom that depends on the circumstances. Look back at Proverbs 28:13. It does not explain what God's mercy looks like in every situation, only that we get it when we openly confess and forsake our sins! It would have been easier if God had given us more detail, but then we might not keep asking and seeking for wisdom.

After a child tells the truth, he may need to make restitution, such as returning a stolen toy. Another child who comes to his parents on his own to confess a wrong may not receive the normal consequence a parent has established for a particular offence, but some natural consequences may need to remain in place. For example, cheating on a test may result in a suspension at school, even if the child confessed; but a parent may determine the suspension is a sufficient consequence, and that no consequences at home are necessary.

Wisdom is not a set of if-then rules. We should not expect to find step-by-step instructions for showing mercy in any book, including the Bible. Rather, wisdom is the application of Scripture to a particular situation. It is a skill that requires practice and reliance on the work of the Holy Spirit.

At every step of our quest to understand mercy, we must pray, seek God, and ask for wisdom as we search the Scriptures to find principles that we can imitate or obey.

1. *Read James 4:8. What are some specific ways that people draw near to God?*

2. *Read James 4:3. Why might prayer, a normally spiritual action, not be effective? How does your answer relate to verse 8?*

3. *What kinds of actions are we hoping our children take as they demonstrate repentance? (Notice the pattern of repentance described in 2 Cor. 7:9-11.)*

Mercy Brings Forgiveness and a Restored Relationship

The crown jewel of God's mercy is the forgiveness that comes through salvation. Before salvation, we were, as the Bible describes, "dead in trespasses": that is, separated from God and unable to reach him ourselves. God, being full of mercy, "made us alive" through Christ. In Ephesians 2, Paul describes this new, living relationship borne out of God's love and mercy.

> *But God, who is rich in mercy, because of His*
> *great love with which He loved us,*
> *even when we were dead in trespasses,*
> *made us alive together with Christ*
> *(by grace you have been saved),*
> *and raised us up together, and made us sit*
> *together in the heavenly places in Christ Jesus,*
> *that in the ages to come He might show the*
> *exceeding riches of His grace in His kindness*
> *toward us in Christ Jesus.*
> *Ephesians 2:4-6*

Paul reminds us that salvation does not come because we are church members, were baptized, because we share our money, or even show mercy to our fellow humans. Salvation is a gift of God that shows off his mercy to insignificant, though very much loved, people. We cannot earn his mercy or his kindness. When we put our trust in Christ alone and call on him for salvation, we receive both God's forgiveness and a new standing as a child of God.

> *For by grace you have been saved through faith,*
> *and that not of yourselves; it is the gift of God,*
> *not of works, lest anyone should boast.*
> *For we are His workmanship, created in Christ*
> *Jesus for good works, which God prepared before-*
> *hand that we should walk in them.*
> *Ephesian 2:7-10*

Understanding that salvation establishes a new relationship with God allows me to think about other ways mercy makes way for forgiveness and a restored relationship. When I am responding to sinful actions of my children, I am sometimes tempted as a parent to hold grudges or offenses without dealing with them properly. Am I forgiving and restoring a close relationship with my children? Am I looking for ways to draw them near to me? Just as God's mercy restores our relationship through forgiveness, I can imitate that pattern with my children.

We need God's help to know each child and know concrete ways to restore a broken relationship. Quiet time away from us might be beneficial to one child but distressing to another. Some toddlers need more reassuring hugs than others. Some children become quite anxious when we correct them. These little ones need lots of reassurance that we love them, even when we correct them. Even our older children are not immune to self doubt when they are corrected or in the process of learning repentance.

We can offer the mercy of a restored relationship after correction in many ways. I have noticed that two of my children tend to withdraw after they have been corrected. Sometimes that time spent alone helps them reconnect later; however, sometimes they end up muttering angry thoughts to themselves, and time alone is not helpful.

My first reaction is to be passive in restoring our relationship, but it is better when I am actively loving them in a way that fits their personality. Sometimes I can say simply, "I love you." Sometimes I can give them space, and then later ask them to join me in a project or an errand. In a quiet moment the next day, I can ask how I can help them do right the next time, or whether I can pray with them. Even if I give them time alone, I am still actively involved in developing that relationship as best as I can.

Above all, my children need to see how God restores relationships when they repent. They need to know that godly correction does not rise out of embarrassment or anger at their misbehavior. I love them even when I do not love their actions. I want them to know that I am on their team, and I'm eager to see what God will do next in their lives.

> *Let the wicked forsake his way, and the unrighteous man his thoughts: and let him return unto the Lord, and he will have mercy upon him; and to our God, for he will abundantly pardon.*
> *Isaiah 55:7*

> *For the Lord your God is gracious and merciful, and will not turn His face from you if you return to Him. 2 Chronicles 30:9b*

4. Read Ephesians 2:4-10. Where is the source of God's mercy, according to verse 4?
5. How would knowing the source of mercy help me show mercy to my children?
6. According to Isaiah 55:7, what is the condition of God's forgiveness and mercy?

Mercy May Modify Consequences

Should my mercy ever result in a change of consequences or discipline for my children? Because I am told to imitate my Heavenly Father, I have found the discussion in Hebrews 12 about God's discipline to be helpful in answering that question.

> *For they indeed for a few days chastened us as seemed best to them, but He for our profit, that we may be partakers of His holiness. Now no chastening seems to be joyful for the present, but*

> *painful; nevertheless, afterward it yields the peaceable fruit of righteousness to those who have been trained by it. Hebrews 12:10-11*

When I remember that the purpose of God's discipline is the "peaceable fruit of righteousness" (Hebrews 12:11), I understand better about my goal for the consequences I give as a parent. When my child repents before I have given consequences, it seems appropriate to reevaluate the consequences I would have given to help them interrupt the sin life-cycle.

Paul illustrates this idea when giving instruction to the church in Corinth: "For if we would judge ourselves, we would not be judged" (1 Corinthians 11:31). This principle holds true elsewhere in the Bible.

Nineveh was a violent society, known for their cruelty to their enemies. Jonah was understandably reluctant to go to Nineveh to give God's message that he planned to destroy their city for its wickedness (Jonah 3). Amazingly, Jonah was not afraid of rejection or personal danger. He was afraid they might actually repent and experience God's mercy!

> *So he prayed to the Lord, and said, "Ah, Lord, was not this what I said when I was still in my country? Therefore I fled previously to Tarshish; for I know that You are a gracious and merciful God,*

Mercy and Repentance 23

*slow to anger and abundant in lovingkindness,
One who relents from doing harm. Therefore now,
O Lord, please take my life from me, for it is better
for me to die than to live!"*
Jonah 4:2-3

When the entire city repented, God changed the consequences and explained how it was merciful to do so.

And should I not pity Nineveh, that great city, in which are more than one hundred and twenty thousand persons who cannot discern between their right hand and their left—and much livestock?" Jonah 4:11

I know from personal experience that repentance does not eliminate all the natural consequences of my sin, but God is often merciful in diminishing the natural consequences of those wrong actions. Not every time that you break the speed limit do you get pulled over by a policeman. I have been lazy and avoided a dirty oven, only to have a friend come over and help me clean. I often experience the natural consequences of my sin, but not always.

Shortening consequences is hard to do as a human parent. We often fear not giving consequences to our children because we fear being "inconsistent" or treating sin lightly. Truthfully, I do not always know when it is merciful to mitigate discipline, but I know that sometimes, mercy simply says, "go and do not sin any more."

I have been particularly perplexed how to respond when there's a mixture of badness and goodness. One day, my son worked half-heartedly on his homework. I reminded him several times to get back on task and at some point, he started working more faithfully. When the task was finished, I was startled to realize I did not want to commend him. After a bit of thinking, I hesitantly decided to tell him how happy I was that he had been faithful.

I think it must be mercy to say, "Well done, thou good and faithful servant" when the job was not perfect. My first inclination was to point out "Except for…." or not consider what he did accomplish, because in my mind, he was distracted about as much as he was not distracted. Still, finishing a job is worth commending. Taking initiative is worth commending.

I have not determined a rule for when I should not commend, but I am looking for how God praises his children. I am regularly asking God to help me praise my children wisely.

Merciful consequences and merciful shortening of consequences should have the same purpose! If shortening consequences results in the peaceable fruit of righteousness, then it's likely we made a wise decision. (Compare

Hebrews 12:5-11 and Romans 2:4.) On the other hand, mercy does mean that God chooses to use painful discipline in some cases. In fact, if we mitigate consequences too often, we may find that we frustrate our children who never know what to expect from us. Or they never learn that sin always has negative consequences, even when we do not see them right away.

> *But if you do not do so, then take note, you have sinned against the Lord; and be sure your sin will find you out. Numbers 32:23*

> *Or do you despise the riches of His goodness, forbearance, and longsuffering, not knowing that the goodness of God leads you to repentance? Romans 2:4*

7. How does the purpose of our discipline ("the peaceable fruit of righteousness") guide us as we decide how to use mercy?

8. Should we inform our children about our plan to show mercy if they come to us before their sin is found out?

9. Can shortening consequences be unmerciful? Explain your answer.

10. Is it sinfully pragmatic to examine the results of our discipline to evaluate it? See Ephesians 6:4.

11. *Can you think of any opportunities you may have to show mercy this week? Write them down in the Chapter 2 action plan.*

3

MERCY AND PATIENCE

For I know that You are a gracious and merciful God, slow to anger and abundant in lovingkindness, One who relents from doing harm. Jonah 4:2a

MAYBE you have heard the statement "Grace is when God gives us something we do not deserve [something good], and mercy is when God does not give us what we do deserve [something bad]." While this aphorism can be somewhat helpful, it can also stifle our understanding of the broad reach of grace and mercy we see in the Bible. For example, in Scripture, mercy is not exclusively

God's withholding painful consequences when I have sinned.

Sometimes God's mercy is a dramatic display of his patience before we repent! Although we see God's merciful patience throughout Scripture, the apostle Paul specifically explains to Timothy that he received mercy so that Jesus Christ might display his perfect patience (1 Timothy 1:16).

God's patience with me gives me time to repent. Several times I've become aware of a sinful habit, and I feel guilty because of my ignorance. I am reminded that I cannot see all the things I need to change at one time. Did God not care about those sins when I did not know about them? Clearly he deals with a limited number of sins that I can handle at one time. I am comforted to consider that God's patience and timing is always perfect (1 Corinthians 10:13, Psalm 130:3-4), even when it comes to dealing with my sin.

> *No temptation has overtaken you except such as is common to man; but God is faithful, who will not allow you to be tempted beyond what you are able, but with the temptation will also make the way of escape, that you may be able to bear it.*
> *1 Corinthians 10:13*

If You, Lord, should mark iniquities,
O Lord, who could stand?
But there is forgiveness with You,
That You may be feared. Psalm 130:3-4

1. How can we show patience to our family members, coworkers, or church family?
2. Is patience always merciful?

Patience Chooses the Right Timing

As I tried to understand and imitate God's mercy, one of the challenges I had was trying to figure out whether it was good to correct every single misbehavior or sin that I saw in my children. My instinct was that if I did not address every sin, then I would be communicating to my children something untrue about God, that God does not care about sin.

Incidentally, many of my friends have expressed this concern as well. It has been helpful for me to remember that God's forbearance in no way minimizes the seriousness of sin. On the contrary, his patience makes way for repentance.

Look again at how God responded to Jonah's sin (Jonah 4). God made a plant to give Jonah shade from the sun. He was not rewarding, or even ignoring Jonah's attitude. Instead, he was gradually revealing the prejudice and selfishness in Jonah's heart. God was not rushed in his timing. He showed mercy both in making the shade, and removing it when Jonah continued to sulk. "I am right to be angry," he pouted.

God gave instruction, correction, and time at each step of discipleship. We never learn about Jonah's ultimate response; we do, however, learn to recognize God's character: gracious and merciful, slow to anger and full of kindness.

A mother may overhear two siblings having an argument. She may choose to listen for awhile to give them an opportunity to resolve the argument, knowing that she can intervene if they continue to have difficulty. She is not waiting because she is indifferent to fighting. Rather, she's giving them an opportunity to choose rightly on their own.

Just like with Jonah, God's merciful patience also gives us time to repent after we have been corrected. I can imitate that patience, too. I sometimes expect my children to wipe away the bad attitude and instantly put on the new attitude, with me watching carefully to see if it's genuine; however, my children often respond far better when I try to help them understand what God expects, and then challenge them to spend some quiet time with God talking to him about the problem. I have noticed when I give them space and privacy, they often surprise me with a righteous response when we talk about it later.

> *For I know that You are a gracious and merciful God, slow to anger and abundant in lovingkindness, One who relents from doing harm.*
> *Jonah 4:2a*

> *Truly, these times of ignorance God overlooked, but now commands all men everywhere to repent. Acts 17:30*

3. What attitude do we expect from our children after we have disciplined them?
4. How might we show mercy when the response is not what we desire?
5. Read Acts 17:30. In what sense does God overlook sin?
6. When might a parent overlook sin in her children in the same way?

PATIENCE WAITS TO DISCERN FULLY

One unexpected result of patience is the perspective that we gain when we are slow to act. Because we are human parents, we have limited knowledge. Particularly with young children who cannot explain themselves, it is wise to observe behavior before immediately responding in correction. Sometimes the child needs further instruction, or time to mature, and sometimes he may change his behavior on his own.

In these cases, by waiting, the parent may discover what to do next. I remember wondering if my 18 month old understood my instruction about throwing his breakfast cereal. I did not really know until I had watched him for a bit to see if I needed to simplify instruction, or repeat it. Did he hear me and understand me? Was he being goofy or resisting a boundary? I was not sure if he needed to be ignored or corrected.

I decided he probably did not hear my instruction and repeated myself. He threw the cereal again. Did waiting backfire? Not at all. We may feel like we have failed when our mercy brings out a negative result, but we actually gain a greater understanding of a child's motives. Sometimes the negative result causes us to reconsider exactly what we hope to accomplish by correction. Either way, our patience helps us to learn better the next step we take. In my case, it seemed clear that my son wasn't hungry any more, and breakfast was over! God gave clarity even when my son's response to patience was not what I expected.

Parents need prayer for discernment to know whether their children understand what they are doing wrong. Age and maturity make a difference in what children understand. Some circumstances or experiences, such as a disability, trauma or prior abuse, may cause a child to respond differently than we expect. Stopping to pray sometimes reminds us to gather more data and personally experience God's mercy before we respond. In all these cases, we can come to God's throne to find the help we need.

> *Let us therefore come boldly to the throne of grace,
> that we may obtain mercy and find grace to help
> in time of need. Hebrews 4:16*

One of my children would laugh when I corrected her. For awhile, her laugh would disturb me, as though she did not realize the gravity of her misbehavior. I reacted harshly until I started to understand that her laughing was actually because she did not know how to interpret her own emotions. She was indeed taking my correction seriously, but I was misinterpreting her response. The longer I observed her behavior, the better I understood her, and I stopped overreacting. As she matured, she stopped laughing when she was corrected.

As children learn what is right and wrong, they tend to demonstrate a guilty conscience in some way. Compare a child who hides from his parents after eating a cookie, or one who brings it to mama to show her the yummy cookie while he's eating it. Just like Adam and Eve hid from God after they sinned, humans have a tendency to hide their actions when they know they are doing wrong.

Showing off is not a foolproof way to determine lack of a guilty conscience, but it can shed light when considered as part of the big picture.

Patience allows me to evaluate whether an event is isolated or becoming a pattern of behavior. I tend to treat discipline as a series of unrelated events, but it is not. Looking at the context over time helps me to decide which negative behaviors to correct. If my daughter forgets her piano books one week, I might bring them to her lesson. If she forgets several times, it may be more merciful to allow her to experience the natural consequences of forgetfulness. If I discover my daughter reading a book instead of cleaning her room, I will respond differently depending on whether she is usually obedient and responsible, or whether I have noticed a pattern of disobedience in this way.

I am thankful that God shows mercy to me as I study my children and learn how to love them better. He reveals when I have acted hastily, and helps me understand when I need a different approach. His patience is a comfort and joy. I can share that!

God's Consequences Are Different When We Sin in Ignorance

God's mercy can result in consequences far less severe than our sin might deserve. As we attempt to imitate God, we must learn why and when this response happens.

Ignorance of the rules is a possible reason for this kind of mercy.

> *Although I was formerly a blasphemer, a persecutor, and an insolent man; but I obtained mercy because I did it ignorantly in unbelief.*
> *1 Timothy 1:13*

In Paul's case, he thought he was pleasing God when he persecuted Christians. God showed him mercy and taught him otherwise. We can imitate this approach when we show mercy to children who "should know better" but don't, especially if there has not been clear instruction in the first place.

Because we are human and imperfect, we do not always clearly instruct our children. Just as our knowledge of God's law helps us know what is important to God (Romans 7:7), parents give instruction so their children understand what is expected of them. "I would not have known sin except through the law." Sometimes, however, we assume our children know what is right and wrong when they do not.

When a child is young, parents identify broad categories: obedience, truth telling, kindness. We think once we define *kindness*, our children can identify it easily, and will know when they are not kind. In fact, parents continually add to the understanding of their children. Pulling the dog's tail is not kind. Teasing a sibling can be kind, but not always. When our children do not know what they are doing wrong, mercy is appropriate. They are still learning how to listen to their conscience, still expanding their definitions of goodness.

Occasionally, the ignorance of our children is a lack of knowledge, but not sin. When my son burnt a hole in one of my tablecloths while soldering, I responded by asking him to please remove the tablecloth, and use a mat in the future. If he burns another hole in a tablecloth, I'll probably be asking him to replace it. Soldering on my tablecloth was not a sin. I had not given him "soldering in the kitchen" guidelines. Sometimes we impulsively treat events like these as sins because someone gets hurt or property is damaged; however, mercy causes us to slow down and use wisdom in our response.

Slowing down helps us discern how to respond to forgetfulness as well. Can or should a parent show mercy to a forgetful child? Sometimes it is more merciful to allow our children to experience the consequences of their forgetfulness. Furthermore, forgetfulness is often the result of deliberate choices to value the wrong things: I remember the things that are important to me. At the same time, we sense that forgetting is often not the same as deliberate defiance. A child who is actively trying to remember may need mercy and help figuring out ways to be more responsible. This kind of help takes time, and kind patience, as we respond.

※

7. *How do parents expand a definition of obedience for their children as they get older? (i.e., "Obedience is doing what mommy says, but also _____.")*

8. *In what way does Ephesians 4:25 expand our understanding of lying? (i.e., "Lying is saying untrue things, but also _____.")*

9. *As we read the Bible, how does our own understanding of how to be right with God change and grow?*

Examining the Heart

Learning to be merciful may result in some paralysis instead of patience! When a parent begins to consider the sufficiency of his instruction, he can become discouraged because it is impossible to be perfectly precise and sufficiently clear at all times for our children. My children have sometimes brought up a loophole or vague instruction as a reason for their misbehavior, and for awhile, I was unsure what to do!

Over time, I have learned more confidence when I respond. They must ask for clarification if they are not sure how to obey. If they know what a teacher or parent *means*, then they must not use imprecision as an excuse to disobey.

King David demonstrates a carefulness and concern about sins of ignorance when he asks God for help avoiding them. "Cleanse me from secret faults" (Psalm 19:12). He asks for help to remember what is right. This is the attitude we want to cultivate in ourselves and our children.

In contrast, "presumptuous sins" are those sins that a person knows are wrong, but chooses them anyway. Numbers 15:17-31 distinguishes sins of ignorance, and sins of presumption. These verses do not prescribe consequences for parents to follow, but they do indicate that God recognizes a difference between intentional and unintentional actions. We learn that, in our discipline, defiance and deliberate disobedience should be treated more seriously than other types of wrong doing.

While the Bible suggests that mercy is appropriate in some measure because of our ignorance, we must still take care about actions that displease God. We take the time to read the Bible so we know what pleases him. Listen to King David's passionate desire to be right with God:

> *How can a young man cleanse his way?*
> *By taking heed according to Your word.*
> *With my whole heart I have sought You;*
> *Oh, let me not wander*
> *from Your commandments!*
> *Your word I have hidden in my heart,*

> *That I might not sin against You.*
> *Psalm 119:9-11*

I am thankful for God's mercy to me when I have been unaware of the seriousness of my sin, and I can imitate that mercy with my children. This mercy is not at all at odds with teaching them to love God's commands and to seek him and please him in all we do.

> *'But the person who does anything presumptuously, whether he is native-born or a stranger, that one brings reproach on the Lord, and he shall be cut off from among his people. Because he has despised the word of the Lord, and has broken His commandment, that person shall be completely cut off; his guilt shall be upon him.'*
> *Numbers 15:30-31*

10. According to Numbers 15:31, why are presumptuous sins taken so seriously?

11. What are some ways that parents can distinguish between sins of ignorance and sins of presumption?

12. Have you experienced mercy from an authority when you violated a rule unintentionally? How might your actions be different than violating a rule because you did not take rules seriously? Does the difference justify a different consequence?

And that servant who knew his master's will, and did not prepare himself or do according to his will, shall be beaten with many stripes. But he who did not know, yet committed things deserving of stripes, shall be beaten with few. For everyone to whom much is given, from him much will be required; and to whom much has been committed, of him they will ask the more.
Luke 12:47-48

13. Read Luke 12:47-48. Why do you think the servant who did not know the rules was still punished?

4

Mercy
When I Am Offended

Thus says the Lord of hosts: "Execute true justice. Show mercy and compassion everyone to his brother." Zechariah 7:9

Sometimes we find it hard to sort out the best way to show mercy because the situation affects us emotionally. Up until this point, we have been thinking about mercy clinically as an action that interrupts discipline or changes a consequence. Actual situations that require mercy are dynamic and often emotional, so we don't always act the same under these circumstances as we imagine we would in a hypothetical and unemotional scenario. In this chapter, we will consider passages in the Bible that describe showing mercy in the midst of personal offense. These passages help us understand why showing mercy can be so difficult, and why we desperately need wisdom and divine help from the Holy Spirit.

> *But love your enemies, do good, and lend, hoping for nothing in return; and your reward will be great, and you will be sons of the Most High. For He is kind to the unthankful and evil. Therefore be merciful, just as your Father also is merciful.*
> Luke 6:35-36

Notice that the mercy described here seems separate from an expectation of repentance: "hoping for nothing in return." God is kind to the unthankful and evil. In this context, God's kindness is not dependent on a person's actions. The mercy described in this passage is not a specific mercy in response to sin.

Can this passage apply to parenting? Is God asking the tired, hard-working mother to smile passively as her children demand everything and show gratitude for nothing? Not at all. God is not talking here about how to teach thankfulness. We find in this passage an example of God's character, setting the tone for how I teach my children thankfulness. God's kindness to the unthankful can help us navigate our responses to the unthankful, too.

Kindness When I Correct My Child

As a father pities his children, So the Lord pities those who fear Him. For He knows our frame; He remembers that we are dust.
Psalm 103:13-14

Kindness when our children are unthankful or in some way undeserving is difficult because I am tempted to be irritated and sarcastic when I correct them. I want to take away all their blessings and see how thankful they are when they are suffering. This anger sometimes causes me to respond with a vengeful spirit that is more harsh than is kind, even when I know better. "I sacrifice, and they are oblivious to what I do for them! How does it make sense to respond with kindness to those attitudes?"

My instinctive emotional response is not always the best one (understatement of the year). I may be expecting a good response or appreciation, but my mercy is not a contractual act, where my children are required to respond in a certain way. Regardless of their response, if I cannot be kind when I teach or correct, then I am not following God's example.

God is kind to the unthankful and the evil. The Holy Spirit reminds me that I am responsible to show kindness, and not to force repentance! We also remember that discipline is not an excuse for treating our children with contempt or rudeness. No matter how we teach and correct our children, no matter what our personality, we all must follow God's example. He is our perfect Father.

When I do correct with this divine perspective, the difference is profound. I nudge them in the right direction rather than react out of proportion to the offence. When I use humor, I am more gentle and less sarcastic. I act more thoughtfully and less impulsively.

Sometimes adjusting blessings and encouraging responsibility help children learn thankfulness better than our words of correction alone. Earlier last year I noticed a growing amount of complaining about lunch. Sometimes I made lunch an hour or two later than someone wanted, and sometimes what I made was not always to everyone's liking. In response, I was getting grumpy and not feeling like making them anything. When I stopped to consider that my words were not changing their attitudes, I realized some practical changes would help my children better than my lectures. I bought a few simple and colorful lunch cookbooks and told them that I was putting them in charge of their own lunches. I'd be happy to purchase ingredients, or convenience foods (within reason), but they were now on their own. My solution has not been without the need for followup. They sometimes attempt a lunch and need another hand. Sometimes they do not clean up as they should. The good news is, when I do make lunch, they seem more thankful. In retrospect, giving responsibility ended up being a merciful tool to teach them thankfulness in this situation.

God seems to give me many opportunities for mercy at the dinner table! Several times I have been tempted to bristle when a child asked what I was making for dinner, and then in the next breath declared the meal undesirable. I'd like to say, "Tough. You can go to bed without supper if you don't like it." A kinder approach would be to say "Wait until you've tried it." Other times I've told them not to tell me their opinion until after dinner or if they have been asked. They are learning!

We think of mercy in big offenses, but often our mercy leads to small and practical actions or shifts in tone. He is kind to the unthankful, and I can be, too.

Kindness When I Do Not Correct

Have you ever had a friend act selfishly, or thoughtlessly? Maybe you are careful about exposing your child to sickness, and your friend comes to a play date, forgetting to mention her baby was throwing up the night before. Perhaps she asked for a favor that caused quite a bit of inconvenience, and then never said thank you. In situations like these, you may have had to choose whether to bring up the offense or to let it go.

We often help our children navigate this same kind of scenario with each other. They may get bumped in the hallway, and instantly assume a sinister motive. We do not expect them to correct each other every time one offends the other! We know that our children will be much happier if they can overlook a great majority of unintentional slights or rudeness from others.

As parents, we should recognize that many thoughtless comments by our children are not really those that need to be addressed, either. Thankfully, using God's mercy as a reference point helps me avoid the self condemnation that comes if I do not correct every time I see bad behavior.

Although God tells me to be thankful in all things, more often than not I live my life blissfully unaware of the innumerable ways God showers me with kindness. We see through a dark glass; we cannot comprehend the depth of God's lovingkindness.

If I were to correct my children every time they were selfish or unthankful, I'd be talking non-stop and would crush their spirits. There is a limit to how much our children can handle correction about thankfulness.

Mercy When I Am Offended

If You, Lord, should mark iniquities, O Lord, who could stand? But there is forgiveness with You, That You may be feared.
Psalm 130:3-4

Many times God's lovingkindness goes unrecognized until years later. In my immaturity, I have experienced many blessings that I was unaware of and thus unthankful for. I have felt at times that God has withheld something good from me. With time, and the perspective of Scripture, comes gradual understanding and greater trust and thankfulness.

For the Lord God is a sun and shield; The Lord will give grace and glory; No good thing will He withhold From those who walk uprightly. O Lord of hosts, Blessed is the man who trusts in You! Psalm 84:11-12

One season comes to mind. Because of my husband's job in the military, we have had opportunities to be in a variety of churches. In one of our places, I was praying earnestly for godly friends for my son. I envisioned godly teenagers that my son could look up to. Instead of the answer to prayer I was expecting, all the mothers I met had girls (who played with my daughters) or boys much younger than my son. At one point, he joked that his best friend was a two year old. My heart chafed, but it was not until several years later that I saw my son developing leadership traits because of his friend dynamic. He started seeing himself as a leader in a way I had not seen developing before. I have a bigger understanding of God's kindness, and now my heart is thankful. God did not withdraw the blessing of young friends in indignation when I was ungrateful. He is kind to the unthankful.

> *The discretion of a man makes him slow to anger,*
> *and his glory is to overlook a transgression.*
> *Proverbs 19:11*

1. *Is it possible to explain to our children how much we do and sacrifice for them? If we could tell them, would they understand it?*
2. *Why might a parent fear that kindness will undermine her efforts to teach her children? How does imitating God's mercy answer this fear?*

Pray for Those Who Are Undeserving

Jesus' prayer on the cross for his enemies is a practical example of kindness to the unthankful and evil. Why was he asking for mercy to be shown to them? "Because they do not know what they do" (Luke 23:34). Yes, their actions were evil and sinful, but they were blind to whom they were murdering. That blindness caused Jesus to pray for them with compassion and pity.

Actually, the mindset required for mercy is identical to the mindset required for praying for our enemies. If we are to treat our enemies with kindness, prayer, and mercy, how much more should we treat our children this way when they behave like a hostile enemy?

I have found that when I pray for my children, and see their weaknesses from an eternal perspective, I am more patient and merciful with them as I teach them what is right. Prayer allows me to keep my emotions under control even if my correction doesn't seem merciful.

> *But I say to you, love your enemies, bless those who curse you, do good to those who hate you, and pray for those who spitefully use you and persecute you, that you may be sons of your Father in heaven; for He makes His sun rise on the evil and on the good, and sends rain on the just and on the unjust. Matthew 5:44-45*

3. Compare Matthew 5:44-45 and Luke 6:35-36. What ideas do both of these passages have in common?

4. Does it make sense to apply Jesus' instructions on loving enemies to how we treat our children? Why or why not?

A Gentle Response to Immaturity

One of my favorite verses reminds me that God is a gentle shepherd, particularly for those who need extra care. I love this beautiful word picture of a shepherd carrying weary lambs, and slowing down for those who need just a little bit more time than others. At times, we all feel weak and unable to keep up spiritually. God knows when we are at our limit. He carries us close to his heart.

> *He will feed His flock like a shepherd; He will gather the lambs with His arm, And carry them in His bosom, And gently lead those who are with young. Isaiah 40:11*

God's mercy gently slows me down when my children's immaturity is annoying or personally embarrassing. The speed of a toddler or the emotions of a teenager are irritating if we do not accommodate their God-given pace!

If I recognize when my children's endurance for good behavior is at a limit, I will be more merciful when they are tired. One afternoon at a park, I watched a daddy tell his young daughter it was time to go home. She was obviously tired and started to cry. He picked her up, comforting her while he started down the walk towards their car. I loved watching his calm actions that did not overreact or cater to his daughter's tears.

In a similar way, other parents have learned the mercy of giving a five-minute warning before leaving a park or an activity. This accommodation is not catering to a sin nature, but mercifully understanding the limitations of a child's mind and difficulty with transitions.

Mercy doesn't rush maturity. Many behaviors mend themselves with time or minimal direction. For example, while I am teaching my children to be humble, I still recognize that in their immaturity, they can brag to try to carry on a conversation, to make friends, and to cover up fears. I can resist the temptation to be disgusted at their bragging, and instead deal with it in the greater context of young people learning to negotiate the social world around them. In the course of positive instruction, the immaturity often takes care of itself.

Children are acutely sensitive to compassion. Whether we respond to their immaturity with forbearance or specific direction, let us follow in our gentle shepherd's example.

5. *How is God like a gentle shepherd in your life?*
6. *How can we imitate this gentleness in our discipleship relationships?*

Transparency Is a Surprising Help for Mercy

Or how can you say to your brother, 'Brother, let me remove the speck that is in your eye,' when you yourself do not see the plank that is in your own eye? Hypocrite! First remove the plank from your own eye, and then you will see clearly to remove the speck that is in your brother's eye.
Luke 6:41-42

Watching my children's weaknesses is like looking into the window of my own soul. That discomfort I feel can cause me to overreact because I know the grief of my own sin. I come to realize that the catchy Christian slogans I share with them are not even changing me. I tell them to trust God without knowing myself how to stop worrying about my problems. I nag them about their lack of self control while I compulsively raid the refrigerator. I might suggest they walk in the spirit, and their blank response helps me to realize that I do not know what that phrase means either. Then I am driven to learn and understand, so that I can help us both.

In many cases, showing mercy means talking about the lessons God is teaching me. I tell my children that I also find it hard to obey when I do not understand or like what God has said. I, too, have had to trust God when I obey him. Gentleness means that I do not spend a long time lecturing!

Sometimes, as I try to figure out how to be merciful to my children, I discover something that I need to change in my own life (Luke 6:41). Actually, my children's spiritual needs have so frequently driven me to understand God's word better, I cannot help but thank the Lord for his ingenious and merciful method of teaching me through my children.

7. *In Luke 6:41-42, what is the behavior that Jesus calls hypocritical?*

8. *What benefit does Jesus identify when we remove the plank from our own eyes?*

9. *Are there any areas where you might need to slow down or show compassion with your children this week? Write them down in the Chapter 4 action plan.*

5

Mercy and Meeting Needs

So which of these three do you think was neighbor to him who fell among the thieves?" And he said, "He who showed mercy on him." Then Jesus said to him, "Go and do likewise." Luke 10:36-37

The story of the Good Samaritan highlights what it might look like for one person to show mercy to another, simply because it is needed. Many of the examples from the Bible that we have looked at identify mercy as an action that is shown in response to, or in spite of, sin. Beyond this usage, the Bible also uses the word *mercy* to mean simply, meeting a need. All we need are eyes to see the needs!

The Samaritan with physical resources met the physical needs of one who was helpless. We imitate this practical mercy by considering and meeting the needs of those around us, including our children. The generosity we see in the good Samaritan should spill out of our lives, too.

A baby is not sinning when she cries out of boredom to be held, but she is expressing a helplessness that we can meet. Holding her and cuddling with her can absolutely be merciful. Our children often fear silly things, and often seem unreasonably emotional. We may be tempted to dismiss their fears or correct their immaturity; however, when we meet their needs practically with a night-light, or a hug and kind words, we are imitating our Heavenly Father's kind of mercy.

Sometimes we are generous naturally, but often we are not. We may not notice the needs around us. Or we may see so many needs we do not know where to start! We are absorbed with our own problems, not realizing that God often ministers to our needs while we meet the specific needs of others. We are so good at identifying when mercy should *not* be shown, that we may end up never showing mercy at all!

I often lack mercy when I do not feel like helping, or when it is inconvenient to help. Sometimes my children ask for help, and I suspect my help is not needed or is undeserved. I need wisdom to interpret these situations and respond appropriately. Meditating on God's mercy will give motivation as well as direction in meeting these physical needs.

1. In what practical ways did the Samaritan show mercy to the injured man? (If you are unfamiliar with this story, you will find it in Luke 10:25-37.)

Wisdom to Evaluate Our Priorities

He has shown you, O man, what is good;
And what does the Lord require of you
But to do justly, To love mercy,
And to walk humbly with your God?
Micah 6:8

Mercy often requires me to subordinate my desires to my children's needs, a higher priority. We may dread the hidden, tedious moments of parenthood: changing diapers, folding laundry, and reminding children to pick up after themselves. These do not feel like godliness and mercy, but each decision to sacrifice and serve is counted as mercy.

Meeting basic needs may be tiresome, but meals continue to be made, dishes washed, and children cared for. We do not meet these needs because we are a special type of person or have a particularly nurturing personality; we meet them because we love our children. When we are tempted to consider the sacrifices of a parent as trivial, we can find encouragement to know that such mercy is precious to God (Micah 6:8).

The more insignificant we consider a need, however, the more difficult it becomes to interrupt our plans or goals. Some interactions are certainly less important, a mixture of want and need that may or may not be given: a birthday present for every childhood friend, a new Easter dress every year, or sports for each child in the family every year. Children want to explain their latest Lego creation or fishing technique. They want us to play a board game with them, or talk after bedtime. Good parents routinely put their own desires aside for the benefit of their children, but they do not always know immediately the most loving action to take.

We have all experienced disappointing times where we needed help, and people were too busy to meet the need. If they had known the need was urgent, perhaps they would have helped. We can do the exact same thing to our children, if we are not careful, especially when they are not bleeding or do not have a life-threatening problem. If I am on my computer, I have to deliberately put it away when my children ask for my attention. I have learned it is merciful to take a pot off the fire when I am interrupted during cooking. Most things on the stove can handle a brief time off the fire, and that way I can pay attention to the need without the distraction of burning food. It is not always merciful to stop what I am doing to help, but often it is.

Exercising wisdom in determining when to show mercy is one way that we grow in learning.

> *Behold, the third time I am ready to come to you; and I will not be burdensome to you: for I seek not yours but you: for the children ought not to lay up for the parents, but the parents for the children. And I will very gladly spend and be spent for you; though the more abundantly I love you, the less I be loved.*
> *2 Corinthians 12:14-15*

> *But we were gentle among you, just as a nursing mother cherishes her own children. So, affectionately longing for you, we were well pleased to impart to you not only the gospel of God, but also our own lives, because you had become dear to us. 1 Thessalonians 2:7-8*

2. *Read 2 Corinthians 12:14-15 and 1 Thessalonians 2:7-8. How does Paul exemplify the sacrificial love of a parent?*

Wisdom to Discern the Need

Helping people is sometimes straightforward. If a child falls off his bike and breaks an arm, we do not have to ponder whether a trip to the doctor would be merciful or not. In reality, mercy is not always so obvious! When it comes to deliberately practicing mercy on a daily basis, we experience a great deal of ambiguity that must be sorted, and sometimes accepted.

Our children do not always know what they need. Sometimes they need help and ask in a clumsy or immature way, and sometimes they do not ask for help at all. In these cases, I must look back to God as my reference point if I am to be merciful as he is merciful.

I do not always know what I need, either! I recognize this lack of awareness in myself when I look at God's word. The Holy Spirit understands my true needs, and promises to translate my awkward or misdirected prayers.

> *Likewise the Spirit also helps in our weaknesses. For we do not know what we should pray for as we ought, but the Spirit Himself makes intercession for us with groanings which cannot be uttered. Romans 8:26*

Mercy and Meeting Needs

Because humans are not omniscient, we will often need to act with partial information. A typical question we ask ourselves is whether help is truly needed, but often a need for help is more than just a child's inability to complete a task.

When my husband was gone on a deployment, I asked for help getting our sprinkler system back in order after winter. When the person I asked declined and responded that the manual was probably at the house somewhere, I spent a long time thinking about why I had asked for help doing something I admittedly could have figured out on my own. I finally concluded that I wanted someone to share my burden. I was not asking for help because I was incapable of figuring out the sprinkler system. I had three children under four years old, and I was managing other things. I vowed that I would remember not to assume a request for help was only legitimate when I perceived a person was completely incapable of accomplishing the job.

That single mom? She is capable of getting all her kids to their sporting events, but maybe one child needs more mom time and she cannot do that without help. The parents who need counseling to know how to help their daughter? Sure they might muddle through on their own, but getting help is not only about ability. That friend who called to ask about a resource for a financial question? She could have googled it, but she needed a listening ear and compassion, too. No matter how competent we may be, God designed us to grow in community.

Now I am wondering whether my experience might help me when my children ask for help. I might resist showing mercy because I know they do not really need my help, but what if they need my presence more than assistance? What if assistance was the way we give our presence? I'm thinking how many times in the Bible we read "I will be with you" or "I will not leave you." God's reassuring presence is associated with his mercy and help.

> *When you are in distress, and all these things come upon you in the latter days, when you turn to the Lord your God and obey His voice (for the Lord your God is a merciful God), He will not forsake you nor destroy you, nor forget the covenant of your fathers which He swore to them. Deuteronomy 4:30-31*

> *Have I not commanded you? Be strong and of good courage; do not be afraid, nor be dismayed, for the Lord your God is with you wherever you go. Joshua 1:9*

3. How is God's presence evidence of mercy?

4. *Can you think of a time when someone's presence was helpful to you? In what ways do our children desire our presence?*

Mercy and the Power of Teamwork

Knowing that a request for help involves more than actual help can lead me to meet the need while still encouraging my child to grow and develop independence. I can come to the kitchen to start dinner when my child asks for help making cookies. "I think you can do this on your own, but I will help you if you get stuck." I can sit beside my daughter when she is overwhelmed by math homework. "Read it out loud. I will help you if you cannot figure it out." Offering our presence is a way to show mercy without creating an unhealthy dependence.

However, our presence is not always sufficient help. We regularly try to help our children accomplish a task while also encouraging them to learn good independent habits. Some children begin well, but lose heart before the job is finished. Their ability to finish the job is weak, especially when the task is large. Helping a child finish teaches him that finishing the job is important. Mercy helps him to receive the satisfaction of accomplishing a large goal that he might not have finished on his own. Other children struggle to start a task. Mercy gets this child started, and then backs off once they have some momentum.

We are not always sure of the best way to meet our children's needs, and our mercy may not end up the way we expect. In those cases, we make the best choice we can with the knowledge we have at that moment, and leave the results in God's merciful hands.

When our son put off mowing the lawn, and we experienced several days of rain and quick growing grass, he ended up with a job that was overwhelming. He was out working hard, but the job was taking far more time than normal. My husband went out to help him finish the job. When I asked our son what made his dad's help merciful, he answered "because I didn't want to do the job." I was dismayed and confused. He failed to connect his irresponsibility and the kindness of his dad's help. Did that make the help an unwise way to show mercy? Should we be helping our children understand why exactly they need mercy? Or is their response helpful in determining how to respond next time? I felt like a mercy-giving failure!

As I look back on this incident, I realize that these questions are normal and a part of wisely assessing our mercy giving. I was overthinking mercy. My son will have opportunities to experience the consequence of procrastination in the future, but other circumstances made the job significantly harder and overwhelming. I was thinking "mercy will fix your sin" but his dad kindly realized that the job would be easier with someone to come alongside him.

Mercy and Meeting Needs

5. *Read Mark 9:23-27. How did Jesus respond when the father asks for mercy and expresses his weak faith?*

6. *How did Jesus respond to the disciples' questions about their failure? Was his answer merciful?*

A Time to Teach, a Time to Help

Lecturing comes easy for parents, but our desire as parents to teach and shape our children's lives sometimes causes us to teach unmercifully. Consider the principle of 1 Corinthians 10:13 when deciding when to stop talking, and when to step in and start helping.

> *No temptation has overtaken you except such as is common to man; but God is faithful, who will not allow you to be tempted beyond what you are able, but with the temptation will also make the way of escape, that you may be able to bear it.*
> *1 Corinthians 10:13*

After a morning repeatedly correcting my daughter for leaving toys and clothes wherever she lost her train of thought, I noticed she had left her plate at the table after lunch. Instead of calling her to get it, I figured she had heard enough of my corrections that morning, and put it away without commenting. I was deliberately trying to apply 1 Corinthians 10:13 to the situation.

In this passage, Paul highlights God's faithfulness: because he is faithful, we can be confident he will not give us some trial and then forget about us. He stretches us exactly to the point we need, and he always makes an escape if it is needed. Similarly, when we as parents ask our children to do hard things, we consider whether we are asking them something beyond their ability to handle at that moment.

I remember when I was young and trying to deal with problems late at night, my mom would say, "Go to bed, Michelle. It will be better in the morning and we can talk about it then." My mom was imitating God's faithful mercy when she knew I was too tired to think rationally and sent me to bed. Morning was a much better teaching time for me.

A time restraint may also be a part of discerning when to help more than teach. Often a child is working more slowly than I like, or more slowly than he is capable. I am more likely to discipline in anger and irritation when I am feeling pressure, and I have discovered these are not great times for teaching or making a point about working efficiently. Helping is often a more merciful approach. We can talk about what led to the need at a less emotional time.

When my son could not find his AWANA Bible memory book in his messy room, I made the choice to help him look (even though he was not looking very thoroughly), and chose not to lecture him about his messy room, the need to put books away properly, or his inefficient searching. My son's need was not life-threatening, but he may not have found the book before we needed to leave for church. How often do I neglect to help when I'm pressured for time, instead taking up time to lecture?

God knows the limits of our endurance. We do not always know our children's limits, but we still should attempt to adjust to them as best as we can. The times when I have gotten it wrong are many. I've pushed too hard only to watch a child burst into tears and withdraw. As I become more sensitive, those times are not as many. When they cry, believing I am not acting mercifully, I can show kindness even if I am unable to help them see my point of view. Ultimately, God's character gives me a goal to shoot for as I seek to show mercy like he does.

Responding to Imperfection

As a father pities his children, So the Lord pities those who fear Him. For He knows our frame; He remembers that we are dust.
Psalm 103:13-14

When my children were young, I found it relatively easy to show mercy when a job was not done perfectly. As they have grown older and more capable, I have noticed I struggle more knowing how much imperfection to allow.

The ways I show mercy have changed. Where I might have overlooked a chore done imperfectly when they were younger, I have gradually changed how much imperfection I allow. I did not expect my four year old to sweep like an adult. I would regularly commend his work, and then sweep after him, knowing the quality of his work would improve. As my children grew older, I expected more from them. I noticed them getting irritated by my maturing expectations for their work, and I had to stop to explain that my expectations were actually changing.

I wish I had figured out a graceful way to transition during that process, but explaining how my expectations changed with their physical development did help them.

I am learning how mercy allows imperfection, even with my older children. Immaturity is not sin. "He remembers that we are dust" is a poetic way of reminding us that God is compassionate when we are imperfect and frail.

Consider God's response to Moses grumbling about the weight of his responsibility in Numbers 11:10-17. Rather than giving a rebuke or discipline, God helped Moses solve the problem. We know God corrects complaining and grumbling, but on this occasion something different happened. God told Moses to delegate his responsibility so it was not as overwhelming. In this case, God appears to ignore the grumbling to meet the immediate physical need.

> *If You treat me like this, please kill me here and now—if I have found favor in Your sight—and do not let me see my wretchedness!" So the Lord said to Moses: "Gather to Me seventy men of the elders of Israel, whom you know to be the elders of the people and officers over them; bring them to the tabernacle of meeting, that they may stand there with you.... Numbers 11:16-17*

Just like with Moses, God's lavish kindness is way out of proportion to my feeble awareness of it. I have felt overwhelmed by my failures, too, and have found comfort in God's kindness in those moments. How can I imitate this kindness, regardless of how I respond to misbehavior?

7. *Read 1 Kings 19. List all the ways that God responded in kindness to Elijah's discouragement.*

8. *How does a child's age or emotional state make a difference in how we show mercy?*

Active Listening Is Merciful

The way we communicate with others is a tremendous opportunity to meet needs. Throughout the gospels, Jesus shows us how to communicate with mercy. His questions reveal him as a keen listener. He does not burden his disciples with too much emotional communication. His kind communication style is remarkable, and something we can observe and imitate.

Parents can be like Jesus when they are sensitive to their children's emotional state and respond with kindness, saving a great deal of instruction for later and keeping their words simple. Consider what Jesus says to his disciples when he starts talking about his coming death. "I still have many things to say to you, but you cannot bear them now" (John 16:12). I love these kind words. It is easy for me to miss nonverbal cues from my children showing that they are overloaded with emotion and words. I have a long way to go before I learn the appropriate balance of kindness and brevity, but Jesus shows me that I do not need to cram everything in, and I need to be sensitive to my listeners' emotional state when I speak.

Parents can also imitate the way Jesus asked questions as he served and taught.

> *So He asked his father, "How long has this been happening to him?" And he said, "From childhood. And often he has thrown him both into the fire and into the water to destroy him. But if You can do anything, have compassion on us and help us." Mark 9:21-22*

Jesus' question was not an idle request for information, nor did he need to talk through the problem he was going to solve. Perhaps the question caused the anguished father to think through the extent and nature of his son's need. Most importantly when Jesus asked for the father's story, he was showing that he cared. How often do I interrupt a child because I already know what her problem is and how to fix it? A simple restatement of their words, or a question for more information indicates that I am truly listening: "You are worried because your eye starts hurting when you are looking at small things, is that right? Are your eyes itchy or just tired? Does it happen when you are doing Legos, or just when you are looking at math?" These questions are part of merciful communication.

I often fail to listen well. I may notice my children trying to get my attention when I have time and opportunity to listen. At some point, when I realize they have a need and God starts convicting me about my careless inattention, I can redeem the situation by asking questions. "How does that work? What's happening in this picture? What are you trying to accomplish?" If I catch myself in time, a question is all that's needed. Other times, I have to confess to them that I've not been paying attention and ask for the mercy of repetition. I'm not naturally a good listener, but these moments of self-correction have helped me immensely.

✽

9. *How can we imitate Jesus' kindness shown in John 16:12? Think of different ages we communicate with: newborn, toddler, preschooler, student, young adult.*

10. *When might listening be merciful? When might listening be unmerciful? Write some ideas in your action plan for listening to some topics your children love to talk about.*

6

Discerning Barriers to Mercy

*For I desire mercy and not sacrifice,
and the knowledge of God more than burnt
offerings. Hosea 6:6*

I have been greatly helped by noticing that mercy takes a variety of forms in the Bible. Because I used to think mercy was limited to the reduction of consequences, I have in the past felt like discipline itself is unmerciful, or that mercy in some way undermines justice.

As I have broadened my understanding of mercy, I am growing in my ability to recognize and show mercy in a variety of new ways. The more clearly I understand God's mercy, the more confident I am that I can be a merciful parent, knowing that God is merciful to me when I get it wrong.

Along the way, I have found some barriers to implementing mercy. These barriers are distinct from the trial and error, insecurity, and self-doubt that are a natural part of the growth process. As I timidly attempt to imitate my Heavenly Father, I have learned to expect those hurdles. The barriers, however, prevent me from even trying to give mercy, and with God's help, I will be able to recognize and avoid them.

Pride and a Lack of Mercy

Pride is a barrier that may actually cause us to feel justified in our lack of mercy. In the story of the prodigal son (found in Luke 15:11-32), Jesus' description of the unmerciful elder brother contrasts sharply with the merciful father. This elder brother believes his father's mercy is unjust. He exaggerates his goodness and is at the same time angry at his father's mercy: "I never transgressed your commandment at any time; and yet you never gave me a young goat."

Just as he was unwilling to show mercy to his brother, we can likewise assume that others should not receive God's mercy, either. This assumption places a barrier to giving and receiving mercy that is impossible to overcome. "Blessed are the merciful, for they shall obtain mercy."

Pride makes it difficult to see my own sin and causes me to magnify other people's sins, just like the elder brother did in Jesus' story. Mercy reminds us that we share a sin nature with our children. Mercy overlooks the inappropriate ways my children express their hurt when I have wronged them. Mercy allows me to ask forgiveness without bringing up all their sinful behavior. Mercy corrects with compassion, understanding the tremendous difficulty of denying self. Pride interferes with all of these actions.

As parents, we can pray for humility and spiritual eyes to see our children as our merciful Father does, both eager to restore relationships, and lavish in our compassion.

The stories Jesus told were not for mere entertainment. Jesus understood that the pride of his listeners kept them from both repentance and mercy toward one another. As long as the Pharisees did not see themselves in need of a merciful Savior, they would not come to Jesus for salvation or help. Quoting from the Old Testament, he draws their attention to God's desire of mercy for and from his people.

> *Now it happened, as Jesus sat at the table in the house, that behold, many tax collectors and sinners came and sat down with Him and His disciples. And when the Pharisees saw it, they said to His disciples, "Why does your Teacher eat with tax collectors and sinners?"*
>
> *When Jesus heard that, He said to them, "Those who are well have no need of a physician, but those who are sick. But go and learn what this means: 'I desire mercy and not sacrifice.' For I did not come to call the righteous, but sinners, to repentance." Matthew 9:10-13*

11. Read Matthew 9:10-13. How does the Pharisees' question show their pride? What does their question reveal about their perception of themselves?

In Jesus' story of the prodigal son, the first evidence of the father's mercy was not his eager forgiveness but his willingness to let his younger son leave. Pride causes us to assume inappropriate control over our children's choices, and prevents us from showing this kind of mercy.

Pride is reluctant to allow choice because we think we have a right to exert this control for our own benefit. Children who do not follow Christ are embarrassing. A humble parent will seek to help them learn how to walk with God and cares far less about appearances. I want my children to see God's mercy in action, even if it means that their spiritual weaknesses are more visible to the people around us.

If we control our children's lives to the extent that they never need our mercy, we are robbing them of the opportunity to choose. Instead, we should be allowing growth and autonomy, even if it means that they choose wrongly, just like the prodigal son.

Most importantly, humility allows us to show mercy for God's sake, not because we want model children or because we want others to see our deeds of kindness. As we seek to show mercy, we are confronted with all the ways that God is merciful to us. Appropriating this truth is both humbling and encouraging.

Jesus' teaching in Matthew 6 has profound implications for our parenting and our desire to be seen as good parents.

> *Take heed that you do not do your charitable*
> *deeds before men, to be seen by them.*
> *Otherwise you have no reward*
> *from your Father in heaven.*
> *Therefore, when you do a charitable deed,*
> *do not sound a trumpet before you as the hypo-*
> *crites do in the synagogues and in the streets, that*
> *they may have glory from men.*

*Assuredly, I say to you, they have their reward.
But when you do a charitable deed,
do not let your left hand know what your right
hand is doing, that your charitable deed may be
in secret; and your Father who sees in secret will
Himself reward you openly. Matthew 6:1-4*

12. Read Matthew 6:1-4. How can these verses encourage a mother learning to be merciful and do charitable deeds for her children?

Fear of Being Too Permissive

Fear is another barrier to mercy we may face. We can neglect mercy because we are afraid of communicating that sin is permissible when we show mercy. We fear we are being too lenient, and we suspect that our children will sin more if we show them mercy. Instead of withholding mercy as a visceral reaction, we must look to God's word for help.

Our children may indeed sin more in response to biblical mercy! Even adults have this tendency. In Romans 6, Paul discusses this particular response to God's kindness. He shows the incongruity within those who have received salvation and yet are continuing to live in sin.

*What shall we say then? Shall we continue in
sin that grace may abound? Certainly not! How*

> *shall we who died to sin live any longer in it?*
> Romans 6:1-2

When our children reject mercy and choose to sin, we call them to repentance, just as we see Paul doing. However, their sinful choice does not mean the initial mercy was wrong. Is God's mercy sinful? Certainly not.

Just as Paul warned the Roman Christians about treating God's mercy carelessly, we may need to warn our children that they are treating our mercy carelessly. As a result, it may be necessary to withhold mercy at the next offence so they understand the consequences of their choices. Ultimately, our children are in God's hands, and he is responsible for their repentance and growth, not us, even with perfectly administered consequences and mercy. We have no choice but to trust in God's mercy as we imperfectly seek to reflect his character to our children.

Our children are also fearful that we may be unjust in how we mediate their conflicts, but teaching them to imitate God's mercy can relieve their fears. When one child is unkind, and the second child responds in anger, I have a hard time dealing with both children at the same time. Correcting the original offence seems to communicate that the angry response is justified, but if I correct the sinful response, I appear to be ignoring the unkind behavior. Using the language of mercy helps me teach my children that I am not minimizing sin.

"Will you show mercy to your brother?" Using the Bible's language in this way has made it easier to teach both sides of the conflict at once. Identifying the appropriate response as merciful seems to help them recognize that this kind of mercy is by nature unequal. In a single word, we identify and acknowledge the sin of the offender, and at the same time we elicit the desired response.

We often use the biblical expressions "be kind" or even "show grace"; however, because children have a strong sense of justice, asking them to "show mercy" reminds them that the offence is real, and that parents (and God) are not justifying the offence.

Bearing with one another, and forgiving one another, if anyone has a complaint against another; even as Christ forgave you, so you also must do. Colossians 3:13

1. *In Colossians 3:13, what is the difference between bearing with one another and forgiving one another? What opportunities will you have this week to bear with another believer?*

Fear of Being Too Harsh

Full of a desire to show mercy like my Heavenly Father, I am sometimes thrown into insecurity when my children

Discerning Barriers to Mercy

are unhappy with a decision I have made. They are skilled at appealing for their idea of mercy, and they are often convincing. I start to doubt what mercy is in that situation, and I can quickly slip into fear that I am being unreasonably harsh when they appeal.

When I was young, my parents had occasion to try to help a young adult whose father repeatedly intervened to eliminate consequences for her sin. He argued with her school when she got into trouble. Afraid of being too harsh, he paid fines when she wrote bad checks. He even bailed her out of jail. In the father's mind, allowing her to "suffer" felt wrong and un-Christian. He blamed himself for her behavior, and thus reasoned it was unfair to expect her to face increasingly severe penalties. In fact, it would have been merciful to allow his daughter to deal with the consequences of her sin.

I can see clearly how the father was unmerciful in rescuing his daughter unwisely; however, I am humbled when I recognize my own tendency to cave in when my instruction to my children has been clear, consequences have been understood, and their disobedience is deliberate. Mercy sometimes requires great courage to impose or allow a needed consequence that may affect us personally.

2. *In what way can a parent's misplaced compassion contribute to destructive behaviors in a child?*

A poignant memory has become a reference point in my life, a reminder that loving actions are not always seen as such by the recipient. When my daughter was learning how to crawl, she would see something she wanted, look at me, and then scream. She wanted me to move her the four feet to the desired toy. I recognized that regularly moving her to the toy would not be merciful. Her tears never felt comfortable to me, but I was confident it would not be merciful to give her what she wanted. Knowing that her tears were not always a guide to mercy gave me more confidence in other times when I was not sure what to do.

God's leading does not always feel kind, either. We ask for mercy in a difficult situation, and are discouraged when God does not remove the problem or tell us the future. We want detailed instructions, and God does not parent that way all the time. When we do not feel that God is kind, we must renew our thinking and remind ourselves of what is true.

Jeremiah wrote a poem that illustrates when he felt like God seemed to be against him. On the surface, Lamentations 3 sounds like Jeremiah believes God does not answer prayer, hurts people on a whim, and is generally cruel. Pay attention to the shift from how Jeremiah feels in verses 1-20, to what he knows about God starting in verse 21. "This I recall to my mind, therefore I have hope." Jeremiah dealt with his discouragement by renewing his thinking and reminding himself what he knew was true about God.

All of us will struggle with concerns about being too permissive or too harsh. Our struggle should encourage us to seek the truth of God's word, and to rest in God's mercy as we replace our fear with faithful obedience.

3. *Read Lamentations 3. List the thoughts that give Jeremiah hope.*

4. *Israel felt like God had abandoned her. What is God's answer to that fear in Isaiah 49:14-15?*

> *But Zion said, "The Lord has forsaken me,*
> *And my Lord has forgotten me."*
> *Can a woman forget her nursing child,*
> *And not have compassion on the son of her*
> *womb? Surely they may forget, Yet I will not*
> *forget you. Isaiah 49:14-15*

Fear of Being a Failure

> *The Lord takes pleasure in those who fear Him,*
> *In those who hope in His mercy. Psalm 147:11*

Studying mercy has taught me that even if I fall short when I try to show mercy, God takes pleasure in my efforts to honor him. These mistakes keep me dependent on God and the need to apply wisdom day by day, but they are not evidence of rebellion. One thing has become clear: If I am afraid to show mercy because I do not want to be wrong, I lose an opportunity to learn God's mercy.

Paul teaches us that a passion to know God (Philippians 3:10) develops gradually, and not passively. We are commanded to "grow" in grace and the knowledge of Jesus Christ. A simple garden illustrates the slow, imperceptible change of a plant over time. Likewise, growing in grace and mercy happens gradually, but not without bumps.

If we are not in the habit of receiving God's mercy, the new awareness of our own failure to show mercy can bring a crushing guilt. Thankfully, God gives a remedy. If we have sinned, we can repent of our sin, find rest in his mercy, and thus grow more in our understanding of God's ways. God delights in those who hope in his mercy! His strength is made perfect in our weakness. None of us can brag about our "exceptional mercy skills."

> *Brethren, I do not count myself to have apprehended; but one thing I do, forgetting those things which are behind and reaching forward to those things which are ahead, I press toward the goal for the prize of the upward call of God in Christ Jesus. Philippians 3:13-14*

I find great comfort knowing that God did not give me perfect knowledge as a parent. I sometimes face what feels like failure when I cannot figure out the thoughts of my children: are they truly repentant? Do they really need help? Thankfully, God is helping me gradually grow in my understanding of my children, but he does not expect me to know perfectly what they are thinking! He wants me to act with limited knowledge. Only God is omniscient!

Every day, I have new opportunities to pay attention to what motivates my children, and what discourages them. Every day, I can remind myself that they are loved perfectly by God, who alone knows their hearts. Although I look for evidence that the Holy Spirit is at work in their lives, I must keep in mind that, like a garden, God's work is slow and sometimes imperceptible. We show mercy without knowing the outcome of our action, and the more we work at it, the stronger we become.

Understanding God's mercy and knowing my children require both practice and discernment! This maturity comes from skills developed in the struggle, and our efforts to imitate God's mercy are pleasing to him, even when we do not get it right the first time!

But solid food belongs to those who are of full age, that is, those who by reason of use have their senses exercised to discern both good and evil.
Hebrews 5:14

Other barriers to mercy exist: laziness, anger, an unregenerate heart. Can you identify some barriers in your own life? I find it encouraging to rest in God's promises to lead me as I follow him. If you are troubled by the lack of mercy in your heart, I am confident that God will show you the next spiritual steps to take as you seek him and study his mercy.

> *But He gives more grace. Therefore He says: "God resists the proud, but gives grace to the humble." Therefore submit to God. Resist the devil and he will flee from you. Draw near to God and He will draw near to you. Cleanse your hands, you sinners; and purify your hearts, you double-minded. James 4:6-8*

> *And He said to me, "My grace is sufficient for you, for My strength is made perfect in weakness." Therefore most gladly I will rather boast in my infirmities, that the power of Christ may rest upon me. Therefore I take pleasure in infirmities, in reproaches, in needs, in persecutions, in distresses, for Christ's sake. For when I am weak, then I am strong. 2 Corinthians 12:9-10*

Afterword

The earth, O Lord, is full of Your mercy; teach me Your statutes. Psalm 119:64

It has been fourteen years since I first pondered how to show God's mercy to my son. My children are now entering their teen years, and I still puzzle over mercy verses! I know I have a lot to learn; however, I can see that I am growing in my understanding of mercy as I meditate on God's Word and practice showing mercy to others.

One week, I wrote about all the times when I showed mercy, and when I deliberately did not show mercy, as much as I could remember. Taking the time to think of examples from my own life was a huge help to me. It helped me to grow more aware of mercy. It encouraged me to see how God helped me, and it challenged me knowing that I still had more to learn. Perhaps you will also benefit from sitting down to think of specific examples of mercy in your own life. I think you will be blessed if you try it.

Mostly, I have been challenged to help my children when they did not deserve help, walk them through schoolwork that they could have done without me, praise them for imperfect work, and pick up things that they have left out. I have given consequences, too. Sometimes they do not like the decision I think is best, but I see mercy in all of these actions.

I have noticed as well that I am increasingly burdened to show mercy to people around me, whether at church, in the community, to my neighbors, to Facebook acquaintances, and to people who speed past me on the freeway. Sharing the gospel is vitally important and merciful, but many will not listen unless I am also sharing kindness and love. Regardless of how God calls you to show mercy to your children and neighbors, he intends for all of us to pursue mercy and allow it to characterize our entire lives.

When Jesus taught his disciples, he told them "Blessed are the merciful, for they shall obtain mercy" (Matthew 5:7). In addition to God's mercy that reaches even to the evil and unthankful, Jesus teaches that there is special blessing and mercy given to those who are showing mercy to others. Let us be a merciful people as we show our children the face of our merciful God.

Chapter Summaries and Action Plans

Chapter 1: A Father's Mercy

Hearing the Word

- *Showing mercy is a characteristic of God that Christians are told to imitate. (Luke 6:27-36)*
- *We tend to feel guilty if we do not know why or when or how to show mercy.*
- *We must learn more about God's mercy if we are to imitate it!*
- *Because God commands us to imitate him, he must have given us sufficient knowledge from his word.*

Doing the Word

- *Learn mercy (slowly) by studying and becoming aware of God's mercy. (Matthew 5:7)*
- *Learn mercy (slowly) by giving mercy.*

My action plan this week

-
-
-
-
-

Chapter 2: Mercy and Repentance

Hearing the Word

- *God gives mercy to us when we repent. (Proverbs 28:13, 2 Corinthians 7:9-11)*
- *God's response of mercy includes a restored relationship. (James 4:3-8, Isaiah 55:7, 2 Chronicles 30:9b)*
- *Mercy sometimes means a consequence is modified. (1 Corinthians 11:31, Romans 2:4, Jonah 4:11)*

Doing the Word

- *I must actively work to restore fellowship with my children when they repent.*
- *My response to wrong doing seeks the result of the peaceable fruit of righteousness. (Hebrews 12:11)*
- *I must pray, act, and evaluate whether to modify a consequence in light of this goal.*

My action plan this week

-
-
-
-

Chapter 3: Mercy and Patience

Hearing the Word

- *God's mercy often withholds immediate consequences. (Psalm 130:3-5)*
- *God waits for the best timing. (Acts 17:30)*
- *Because God is patient, I know that choosing patience is not necessarily ignoring sin. (1 Timothy 1:13)*

Doing the Word

- *I can be patient to better understand the actions of my children.*
- *I can choose not to despair when repentance does not come immediately after I correct my children.*
- *I can weigh the offence differently when it is not defiant and deliberate.*

My action plan this week

-
-
-
-
-
-

Chapter 4: Mercy When I Am Offended

Hearing the Word

- *God is gentle with those who need gentleness. (Psalm 103:13-14)*
- *God is kind to the evil and unthankful. (Luke 6:35-36)*
- *This kind of mercy appears separate from a condition of repentance.*

Doing the Word

- *Whether I correct or not, I can imitate God's kindness. (Isaiah 40:11)*
- *I can pray for those who offend me, including my children! (Matthew 5:44)*
- *I can examine my heart to understand my own spiritual needs. (Luke 6:41-42)*

My action plan this week

-
-
-
-
-
-

Chapter 5: Mercy and Meeting Needs

Hearing the Word

- *God's mercy includes meeting needs, not just responding to sin. (Luke 10:25-37; Romans 8:26)*
- *Mercy sometimes requires self sacrifice. (2 Corinthians 12:14-15; 1 Thessalonians 2:7-8)*
- *God's mercy takes immaturity into account. (Psalm 103:13-14; 1 Corinthians 10:13; Numbers 11:16-17)*

Doing the Word

- *I can stop lecturing when I should be listening and asking questions.*
- *I can speak kindly. (James 3:17-18)*
- *I can lead by teamwork. (Joshua 1:9)*

My action plan this week

-
-
-
-
-
-

Chapter 6: Discerning Barriers to Mercy

Hearing the Word

- *God takes pleasure in those who hope in his mercy. (Psalm 147:11)*
- *God wants me to experience and give mercy! (Matthew 9:10-13; Hosea 6:6)*

Doing the Word

- *I can learn to replace fear with faith and obedience. (Philippians 3:13-14)*
- *I can daily replace pride with humility as the Lord reveals my needs through his word and prayer.*
- *I can rest in God's mercy by putting my weaknesses in his creative hands. (Psalm 138:8, Ecclesiastes 3:11)*

My action plan this week

-
-
-
-
-
-

About the Cover

"The heirloom Malabar spinach seeds require tender care in the Midwest as they are slow to germinate and need protection from fluctuating spring temperatures; we start the seeds in the growing shed. The young seedlings are then planted in the soil and trained to climb a trellis. As it grows, the plant vines develop into strong, healthy red stems, twisting and turning in and out of the fences they grow on."
Brynteg Farms, Ashippun, Wisconsin

Cover artist Bretta Watterson used ink to create both the black and white cover wrap of the mature Malabar plant and colorful focus of the seedling. You can find more of her work at https://www.instagram.com/brettabutterfly/

www.ingramcontent.com/pod-product-compliance
Lightning Source LLC
Chambersburg PA
CBHW061337040426
42444CB00011B/2962